KET
Practice Tests

1

TEACHER'S BOOK

Susan McGeary

Richmond PUBLISHING

CONTENTS

INTRODUCTION

This book is intended for students planning to take the UCLES Key English Test – KET – but can also be used, more generally, to test learners who are in their second year of studying English. It provides practice in Paper 1 (Reading and Writing) and Paper 2 (Listening) of the KET test. The five tests in the book are topic related:

Test 1 - Family
Test 2 - School
Test 3 - Home Town
Test 4 - Hobbies and Sports
Test 5 - Jobs

What is KET?

The Key English Test – KET – was developed between 1991 and 1994 and introduced in November 1994. It is a test in three parts intended for students who have studied English for approximately two years or 180 - 200 hours and have a basic competence in Reading, Writing, Listening and Speaking. Each of these skills is tested in KET in three papers – Reading and Writing, Listening and Speaking.

The syllabus

The syllabus for KET is the same as that specified in Waystage 1990 (J.A. van EK and J.L.M. Trim, Council of Europe Press 1991). For a full list of items and exponents teachers are advised to consult that document. However, the following is a summary of the language tested:

Topics

Personal identification
Home, house and environment
Daily life, work and study
Free time, sport and entertainment
Travel and holidays
Relations with other people
Health
Shopping
Food and drink
Services: bank, post office, police, etc.
Places
Language
Weather

Language functions

These fall into six broad categories:
Giving and asking for factual information
Expressing and finding out about attitudes
Getting things done
Socialising
Structuring discourse
Solving communication problems

The structure of KET

KET has three Papers
• Reading and Writing
• Listening
• Speaking

Reading and Writing
70 minutes
50% of marks

Part 1

This consists of ten questions which test candidates' understanding of public signs and notices. Questions 1-5 are 3-part Multiple Choice questions. Questions 6-10 are matching questions.

Part 2

Questions 11-15 test candidates' knowledge of a particular lexical field. Candidates must match a series of words to the appropriate definition.

Part 3

Questions 16-20 are 3-part Multiple Choice questions testing candidates' ability to understand everyday conversations. They must complete 5 separate 2-line dialogues from the 3 choices given.

Questions 21-25 are matching questions. Candidates are asked to complete a longer dialogue from a list of choices.

Part 4

In this part of the test candidates are required to read a text of approximately 180 words and extract the relevant information. Questions 21-26 may be Multiple Choice or candidates may be asked to decide if a given statement is Right, Wrong or whether there is insufficient information in the text to decide.

Part 5

Part 5 is a reading passage followed by five 3-part Multiple Choice questions. It tests candidates' knowledge of grammar and usage, and structural relationships.

Parts 6-8 focus on Writing

Part 6

Part 6 tests candidates' knowledge of grammar and vocabulary. It consists of one or two gapped texts (usually an informal note and a reply to it) which students have to complete.

Part 7

Part 7 is a simple information transfer task. Candidates read a short text and use the information it contains to fill in single words in a form or similar official document.

Part 8

Part 8 tests candidates' ability to produce simple continuous writing in the form of a short note or message, usually to a friend. The instructions specify the kind of note and what information is required.

Listening
25 minutes
25% of marks

The Listening Paper has five parts and a total of 25 questions. The texts are recorded on cassette and each text is heard twice.

Part 1

In part 1 of the paper candidates are required to extract simple factual information from a dialogue. This information could be times, prices, location, shapes, sizes. Questions 1-5 are 3-part Multiple Choice questions based on drawings.

Part 2

In part 2 candidates hear a longer conversation and must extract factual information as in part 1. Questions 6-10 are matching questions for which candidates must match two lists of items.

Part 3

Part 3 is similar to part 2 in that candidates hear a longer conversation and have to extract factual information. However, questions 11-16 are 3-part Multiple Choice questions.

Parts 4 and 5

In parts 4 and 5 candidates are required to write down the information they hear on the cassette. The listening text may be a dialogue or a monologue, for example a recorded message, and candidates are required to listen and fill in a simple form, note or memo with information such as times, dates, prices.

Speaking
8-10 minutes
25% of marks

In the Speaking Paper of KET, candidates are tested in pairs. Two examiners are present: the interlocutor conducts the test, the assessor takes no part in the conversations. The Speaking Paper has two parts:

Part 1

This takes 5-6 minutes, and each candidate in turn talks with the interlocutor giving personal information, for example, name and address, place of origin, occupation, family details.

Part 2

Part 2 takes 3-4 minutes. The two candidates talk to each other asking for and giving personal information about daily life, leisure activities and social life. Prompt cards are used to provide questions.

TEST 1   FAMILY

READING AND WRITING PAPER

Part 1
Questions 1 – 5

Who are these notices for?
For questions 1 – 5, mark A, B or C.

EXAMPLE		ANSWER
0 **DANGER** **CHILDREN CROSSING**	A drivers B children C mothers	A

1   **PLEASE PARK AT THE BACK**

(A)   drivers

B   students

C   conductors

2   **BEWARE OF THE DOG**

A   dog owners

B   people in a restaurant

(C)   everybody

3   **PLEASE CLOSE THE GATE**

A   shoppers

B   passengers

(C)   campers

4   **NO SMOKING**

A   drivers

(B)   customers

C   housewives

5   **Children playing – Be Careful**

A   families

B   housewives

(C)   drivers

Questions 6 – 10

Which notice (A – H) says this (6 – 10)?
For questions 6 – 10, mark the correct letter (A – H).

EXAMPLE	ANSWER
0 Don't wait.	E

6   We won't be long.

7   Your meal is in the cooker.

8   John will telephone again.

9   Take dishes out of dishwasher.

10   Give the dog something to eat.

A   Lunch in oven

B   Put dishes into dishwasher

C   **BACK SOON**

D   John rang again, you have to phone him back

E   We won't be back for a long time

F   John phoned, will ring back later

G   Feed Bruno

H   Empty dishwasher please

Key

6 C   7 A   8 F   9 H   10 G

Part 2
Questions 11 – 15

Read the descriptions (11 – 15) of some rooms in a house.
What is the name of each place (A – H)?
For questions 11 – 15, mark the correct letter (A – H).

EXAMPLE	ANSWER
0 You eat here.	H

11   You sleep here.

12   You wash yourself here.

13   You make meals here.

14   You read and watch TV here.

15   You park your car here.

ROOMS

A   study

B   bedroom

C   garage

D   bathroom

E   hall

F   living room

G   kitchen

H   dining room

Key

11 B   12 D   13 G   14 F   15 C

Part 3
Questions 16 – 20

Complete the five conversations.
For questions 16 – 20, mark A, B or C.

EXAMPLE		ANSWER
0 How many cakes can I have?	A Any. B Three. C No-one.	B

16 Can I go out tonight?

    (A) No, you can't.
    B Tomorrow.
    C At 10 o'clock.

17 What time's lunch?

    A Tomorrow.
    (B) At 1 o'clock.
    C Two hours.

18 Do you want me to lay the table?

    A That's good.
    B No, you don't.
    (C) Yes, please.

19 When will Dad be home?

    A Yesterday.
    B 3 hours.
    (C) Soon.

20 Where's the dog?

    A Into the garden.
    B Yes, he is.
    (C) In the garden.

Questions 21 – 25

Complete the conversation.
For questions 21 – 25, mark the correct letter (A – H).

EXAMPLE		ANSWER
0 Mum:	Where are you, David?	G
David:	0............	

Mum: Where are you going on Saturday night?

David: 21 **C**

Mum: Is it near home?

David: 22 **D**

Mum: What time does it finish?

David: 23 **B**

Mum: That's very late.

David: 24 **F**

Mum: OK, but you must do all your homework on Saturday.

David: 25 **E**

A   That's very late

B   About 2 o'clock in the morning.

C   To the concert. Is that OK?

D   Yes. It's next to our school.

E   I will. Thanks Mum.

F   Please, Mum. You have to let me go. Everyone's going.

G   I'm here, in the kitchen.

H   No, you aren't.

Read the letter that David has written to his friend in Spain.
Are sentences 26 – 32 'Right'? (A) or 'Wrong'? (B).

If there is not enough information to answer 'Right(A) or 'Wrong' (B),
choose 'Doesn't Say' (C).

For questions 26 – 32, mark A, B or C.

David Richardson is fifteen years old and he lives with his family in Manchester.
This is a copy of a letter he wrote to his new pen-pal in Spain.

Dear Juan,

Hello! My name's David and I'm fifteen years old. My birthday is on the thirteenth of March. My mother's name is Christine and she works part-time as a nurse. My father's name is Ted and he works full-time as a company representative. I've got two sisters; one is called Sarah and she's in her last year at school, and the other is called Jenny and she's very naughty. Sarah is seventeen and she's got a boyfriend called John. Jenny is only ten and she always annoys me when I'm studying.

We live in a semi-detached house with a little garden and we have a beautiful cat called Simon. I like playing with my cat but I don't like helping in the garden. Do you live in a house or a flat? Have you got any brothers and sisters? Do both your parents work?

In my next letter I'll tell you about my school.

Write soon.

David

26 David's birthday is on 30th March.

   A Right   (B) Wrong   C Doesn't say

27 His mother works full-time.

   A Right   (B) Wrong   C Doesn't say

28 Sarah is older than David.

   (A) Right   B Wrong   C Doesn't say

29 His father owns a company.

   A Right   (B) Wrong   C Doesn't say

30 They have a small garden.

   (A) Right   B Wrong   C Doesn't say

31 Juan's parents both work.

   A Right   B Wrong   (C) Doesn't say

32 David tells Juan about his school.

   A Right   (B) Wrong   C Doesn't say

Part 5
Questions 33 – 40

Read the article about Life in Britain.
Choose the best word (A, B or C) for each space (33 – 40).
For questions 33 – 40 mark, A, B or C on the answer sheet.

·······LIFE IN BRITAIN·······

Britain has (Example: *some*) customs which are different from other countries, for example, did you know that in Britain most people have __33__ milk delivered __34__ their homes early every morning. __35__ night they put their __36__ milk bottles outside __37__ doors and in the morning the milkman takes the empty milk bottles away and leaves full ones in their place.

You __38__ buy your milk in the supermarket or local shop, if you prefer, but a lot of people __39__ like to have it delivered. The only problem is that __40__ little birds drink some of the milk if you don't cover the bottles or get up very early.

EXAMPLE			ANSWER
0 A Some	B A	C Any	A

33   A his   B its   (C) their

34   A at   (B) to   C in

35   (A) At   B In   C On

36   A full   (B) empty   C tall

37   A our   B his   (C) their

38   A must   (B) can   C have

39   A yet   B already   (C) still

40   (A) sometimes   B ever   C when

Part 6
Questions 41 – 50

Complete the following notes.
Write ONE word for each space (41 – 50).

Dear Michael

I (Example: **am**) sorry I didn't see __41__ yesterday. We're going swimming today __42__ four o'clock. Do you __43__ to come? We __44__ meeting outside the pool.
Bring __45__ money.

See you

David

Dear David,

I __46__ go swimming today. I __47__ got to finish my homework. I went __48__ the cinema last night so I must do __49__ today.
Have __50__ good time!

Michael

Key

41 you   42 at   43 want   44 are   45 some, your
46 can't   47 have   48 to   49 it   50 a

Read this information about a boy who wants to send away for a T-shirt.
Fill in the information on the ORDER FORM.

David Smith is 12 years old and he lives at 17, Windsor
Park, Belfast BT9 6FR. His telephone number is 660502.
He goes to Windsor Park School.
He is very tall and a bit fat. He would like a red T-shirt.

ORDER FORM

First Name:		David
Surname:	51	Smith
Address:	52	17, Windsor Park Belfast
Postal Code:	53	BT9 6FR
Small/Medium/Large:	54	Large
Colour:	55	Red

Part 8
Question 56

You must meet your friend, Peter, after school today.
Write a note to him.

Say:

    why you want to see him
    where and **when** to meet you.

Write 20 – 25 words.

LISTENING PAPER

Part 1
Questions 1 – 5

Listen to the tape
You will hear five short conversations.
You will hear each conversation twice.
There is one question for each conversation.
For questions 1 – 5, put a tick ✓ under the right answer.

Here is an example:

EXAMPLE

What time is the meeting?

20.30   **20.00**   **21.30**

A ✓   B ☐   C ☐

---

1   What time is it?

08.15   **08.50**   **07.45**

A ✓   B ☐   C ☐

2   What does Michael have for breakfast?

Orange Juice   Tea and Toast   Orange Juice
and Toast   and Cornflakes

A ✓   B ☐   C ☐

3   How much money does Michael need?

15p   **50p**   **5p**

A ☐   B ✓   C ☐

4   When is the school concert?

Tuesday   Thursday   Today

A ☐   B ✓   C ☐

5   When is Mary's party?

February 4   February 14   February 5

A ✓   B ☐   C ☐

TAPESCRIPT

Test One

Look at the instructions for Part One.
You will hear five short conversations.
You will hear each conversation twice.
There is one question for each conversation.
For questions 1 – 5, put a tick ✓ under the right answer.

Here is an example:

Example: What time is the meeting?
Mum: What time is the school meeting?
Michael: It's at 8.30.   Are you going?
Mum: Yes, of course.
The answer is 8.30 so there is a tick in box A.
Now we are ready to start
Look at Question 1.

One: What time is it?
Michael: What time is it?
Mum: It's 8.15.
Michael: Oh dear!
Mum: Hurry up or you'll be late.

Now listen again.

Two: What does Michael have for breakfast?
Mum: Do you want tea or orange juice?
Michael: Orange juice please.
Mum: Do you want cornflakes and toast?
Michael: No, just toast please.

Now listen again.

Three: How much money does Michael need?
Michael: I need some money for the bus please.
Mum: How much do you need?
Michael: 50p.
Mum: Here you are.
Michael: Thanks, Mum.

Now listen again.

Four: When is the school concert?
Dad: Is the concert on Tuesday?
Michael: No it isn't.   It's on Thursday.
Dad: Are you playing the guitar?
Michael: Yes, I am.

Now listen again.

Five: When is Mary's party?
Mum: Are you going to Mary's party?
Michael: Perhaps, when is it?
Mum: It's on February 4th at 5 o'clock.
Michael: I don't know.   I'm playing in a football match that day.

Now listen again.

This is the end of Part One.

TAPESCRIPT

Now look at Part Two.

Listen to Nicholas and Lucy talking about their families.
What have each of them got?
For questions 6 – 10, write a letter (A – H) next to each person.
You will hear the conversation twice.

Nicholas: Have you got any brothers or sisters, Lucy?

Lucy: Yes, Nicholas. I have two brothers. What about you?

Nicholas: I have an older sister who is married with two children. Are your brothers married?

Lucy: No, not yet. Alan has a girlfriend and Simon is still studying at university. Simon hasn't got a girlfriend but he has got a dog. I get on very well with him. Do you get on well with your sister?

Nicholas: Yes I do. I like my niece and nephew very much but they are very naughty. My brother-in-law is away quite often so I sometimes help my sister with the children. Her husband is an only child.

Lucy: I would like to meet your family. Can I come with you this weekend and help look after your niece and nephew?

Nicholas: Of course you can. I'll ring my sister and let her know that you are coming.

Now listen again.

This is the end of Part Two.

Part 2
Questions 6 – 10

Listen to Nicholas and Lucy talking about their families.
What have each of them got?
For questions 6 – 10, write a letter (A – H) next to each person.
You will hear the conversation twice.

EXAMPLE	ANSWER
0 Alan	E

PEOPLE

6   Lucy   ☐

7   Nicholas   ☐

8   Simon   ☐

9   Nicholas' sister   ☐

10   Nicholas' brother-in-law   ☐

RELATIVES, ETC

A   Two brothers

B   Two sisters

C   No brothers or sisters

D   A boyfriend

E   A girlfriend

F   A nephew and niece

G   Two children

H   A dog

Key

6 A   **7** F   **8** H   **9** G   **10** C

Part 3
Questions 11 – 15

Listen to Michael talking on the phone to a friend about a trip to see his relatives.

For questions 11 – 15, tick ✓ A, B or C.

You will hear the conversation twice.

EXAMPLE	ANSWER	
0 Michael is going to see	A a friend	☐
	B his cousins	✓
	C his brother	☐

11 Michael is travelling by	A car	☐
	B plane	☐
	C train	✓
12 The journey takes	A 6 hours	✓
	B 8 hours	☐
	C a lot of things	☐
13 He will be met by his	A uncle	✓
	B aunt	☐
	C cousins	☐
14 The weather will be	A dry	☐
	B sunny	☐
	C rainy	✓
15 Michael is going to take	A an umbrella	☐
	B warm clothes	✓
	C a raincoat	☐

TAPESCRIPT

Now look at Part Three.
Listen to Michael talking on the phone to his friend about a trip to see his relatives.
For questions 11 – 15, tick A, B, or C.
You will hear the conversation twice.

Look at questions 11 – 15 now. You have twenty seconds.
Now listen to the conversation.

Edward: Hello

Michael: Hello Edward, it's me, Michael. I'm going to see my cousins next week.

Edward: Oh really, where do they live?

Michael: They live in Scotland and I'm going by train because I don't like the car. I always feel carsick.

Edward: How long is the train journey from London?

Michael: Well, the train leaves at 8.00 in the morning and takes six hours.

Edward: Who will meet you at the station?

Michael: My uncle is going to meet me. My aunt hasn't been well and can't drive.

Edward: What will the weather be like?

Michael: Well, it will be quite cold and wet so I'm going to take some warm clothes to wear.

Edward: Don't forget to take an umbrella!

Michael: It's OK. My uncle said they have lots of umbrellas, so I don't need to take one.

Edward: I hope you have a good journey.

Michael: Thanks a lot, Edward. See you soon. Bye.

Edward: Goodbye.

Now listen again.

This is the end of Part Three

TAPESCRIPT

Now look at Part Four.

Listen to Sarah speaking on the telephone.
She wants to speak to Olive, but she is not there.

Listen and complete questions 16 – 20.
You will hear the conversation twice.

Sarah: Hello. Can I speak to Olive? It's Sarah.

Mother: I'm afraid Olive's not here at the moment

Sarah: Oh dear. Can I leave a message for her?

Mother: Yes, of course.

Sarah: Could you tell her that I've been invited to a wedding

Mother: . . . to a wedding

Sarah: Yes. It's next Thursday, the 13th of April, so I won't be able to go to the beach.

Mother: Oh dear. What time is the wedding?

Sarah: It's at 3 o'clock at St Martin's Church in Hill Road.

Mother: Oh, how lovely. Have you got some new clothes to wear?

Sarah: Yes. Can you tell Olive I've bought a new pink dress and a big, black hat.

Mother: Yes, I'll tell her

Sarah: Oh, yes. Please tell her that the reception is at the Country Club Hotel.

Mother: I will. She'll be very jealous.

Sarah: I'm sure she will.

Mother: Well. Have a lovely time.

Sarah: I will. Thanks. Bye.

Mother: Bye, Sarah.

Now listen again.

This is the end of Part Four.

Part 4
Questions 16 – 20

Listen to Sarah speaking on the telephone.   She wants to speak to Olive, but she is not there.

Listen and complete questions 16 – 20.
You will hear the conversation twice.

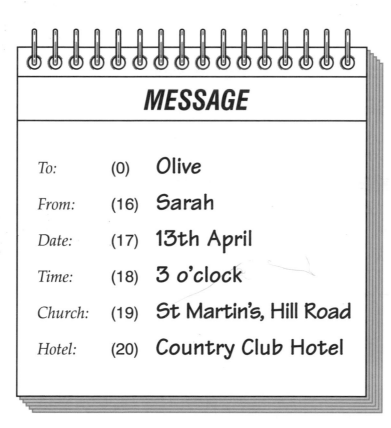

MESSAGE

To:	(0)	Olive
From:	(16)	Sarah
Date:	(17)	13th April
Time:	(18)	3 o'clock
Church:	(19)	St Martin's, Hill Road
Hotel:	(20)	Country Club Hotel

Part 5
Questions 21 – 25

Listen to some information about an adventure park.
For questions 21 – 25, complete the message about the adventure park.
You will hear the information twice.

ADVENTURE WORLD

Opens:		9.00 am
Closes in winter:	(21)	6.00 pm
in summer:	(22)	9.00 pm
Cost for adults:		£8.00
for children:	(23)	£4.00
Young children must be with:	(24)	Parents
For some rides you must be over:	(25)	16 years old

TAPESCRIPT

Now look at Part Five.

You will hear some information about an adventure park.

Listen and complete questions 21 – 25.
You will hear the message twice.

The Adventure World Park is open every day from 9.00 am to 6.00 pm in winter and from 9.00 am to 9.00 pm in summer.
It costs £8.00 for adults and £4.00 for children.
It also costs £4.00 for people over 65 and for students.
A family ticket costs £20.00 for 2 adults and up to 3 children.

Children under 12 must be with their parents.
Please read the notices for each ride carefully. Some are only for people over 16.

We want you to enjoy your day at Adventure World Park, so please help us to make it a safe and happy day.

Now listen again.

This is the end of Part Five.

TEST 2 SCHOOL

READING AND WRITING PAPER

Part 1
Questions 1 – 5

Who are these signs for?
For questions 1 – 5, mark A, B or C.

EXAMPLE		ANSWER
0 **Please don't write on desks**	A people B teachers C pupils	C

1 **SILENCE PLEASE**

(A) students in a library
B students in a classroom
C people in a bookshop

2 Take off your shoes

A students in the corridor
B students in the class
(C) students in the gym

3 No running in playground

A car drivers
B teachers
(C) students

4 Turn off the taps, please

A students
B teachers
(C) everybody

5 *Assembly starts at 9.00am*

A the staff
(B) everybody
C the headmaster

Questions 6 – 10

Which notice (A – H) says this (6 – 10)?
For questions 6 – 10, mark the correct letter (A–H).

EXAMPLE	ANSWER
0 Exams start on Monday	D

6 You can have additional help when normal classes are over.

7 There will be an excursion tomorrow.

8 There is a meeting for teachers tonight.

9 There is a meeting for mothers & fathers this evening.

10 On Friday you have to give back all books.

A Parents' meeting this evening at 8.00 pm

B Extra classes after school

C School trip tomorrow

D Exams begin next week

E The books will be in the bookshop on Friday

F YOU MUST GIVE YOUR NAMES FOR THE EXCURSION TOMORROW

G Please return all books to the library on Friday

H Staff meeting at 8 o'clock this evening

Key

6 B   **7** C   **8** H   **9** A   **10** G

Part 2
Questions 11 – 15

Read the descriptions (11 – 15) of some places in a school.
What is the name of each place (A – H)?
For questions 11 – 15, mark the correct letter (A – H).

EXAMPLE	ANSWER
0 Teachers meet here.	E

11   You can buy your books here.

12   You can read books here.

13   You can eat your school
       lunch here.

14   You can do P.E. here.

15   You meet here in the morning.

ROOMS

A   gym

B   classroom

C   bookshop

D   canteen

E   staff room

F   library

G   kitchen

H   assembly hall

Key

11 C   **12** F   **13** D   **14** A   **15** H

Part 3
Questions 16 – 20

Complete the five conversations.
For questions 16 – 20, mark A, B or C.

EXAMPLE		ANSWER
0 Have I got an English lesson tomorrow?	A Yes, I have. B No, you aren't. C Yes, you have.	C

16 Have we got any homework?

    A Yes, you are.
    B No, there aren't.
    Ⓒ Yes, you have.

17 What time does the exam begin?

    A Last night.
    Ⓑ At 9 o'clock
    C Two days ago.

18 Can you lend me a pencil?

    A Yes, I do.
    Ⓑ Yes, I can.
    C No, I don't.

19 Is there a football match on Saturday?

    A No, it isn't.
    B Yes, it is.
    Ⓒ Yes, there is.

20 Where are the notebooks?

    A Into the cupboard.
    B Onto my desk.
    Ⓒ On my desk.

Questions 21 – 25

Complete the conversation.
What does David say to Simon?
For questions 21 – 25, mark the correct letter (A – H).

EXAMPLE		ANSWER
Simon:	Have you done your Latin homework?	B
David:	0...........	

Simon: Neither have I. Why don't we do it together?

David: 21 **E**

Simon: Shall I come to your house or will you come to mine?

David: 22 **A**

Simon: You live behind the school playground, don't you?

David: 23 **G**

Simon: Well, I'll come to your house at 10.00 in the morning.

David: 24 **F**

Simon: OK. I'll come at 11.00.

David: 25 **H**

A I don't mind.

B Not yet. What about you?

C Neither have I.

D You don't mind.

E That's a good idea.

F That's very early.

G Yes, that's right.

H That's fine. See you tomorrow.

Part 4
Questions 26 – 32

Read the letter David has written to his friend Juan about his school.
Are sentences 26 – 32 'Right' (A) or 'wrong' (B)?

If there is not enough information to answer 'Right' (A) or 'Wrong' (B),
choose 'Doesn't say' (C).

For questions 26 – 32, mark A, B, or C.

Dear Juan,

Our school is called Highfield and it has got 420 pupils, boys and girls. It's the biggest school in Oxford and I think it's the best. It's a comprehensive school so you don't have to pay school fees like you do in the private or "public" schools. (Yes, it's unusual that the top private schools in England are called "public" schools and some foreigners study at them. There are two very famous ones called Eton and Harrow).

As it is such a large school we have wonderful facilities: tennis courts, football pitches, an indoor heated swimming pool, hockey pitches and a snooker room. We also have a good canteen, a language laboratory where I practise my Spanish and French and a modern science laboratory.

We begin school at 9 o'clock in the morning and finish at 3.30 in the afternoon. We only have one hour for lunch which we have in the canteen. A few pupils prefer to bring a packed lunch. After school there are lots of activities such as stamp collecting, chess, theatre etc. In my next letter I'll tell you about my hobbies.
Write soon.

David

P.S. I forgot to tell you my favourite subjects. I prefer languages (I do French, Spanish, English and a little Russian) but I also like history, geography, art and P.E. I don't like chemistry or physics and I hate mathematics. What about you?

26   Highfield is the largest school in Oxford.

(A) Right   B Wrong   C Doesn't Say

27   You have to pay to go to Highfield.

A   Right   (B) Wrong   C Doesn't Say

28   Public schools are free.

A   Right   (B) Wrong   C Doesn't Say

29   The school has an outdoor swimming pool.

A   Right   (B) Wrong   C Doesn't Say

30   Most pupils eat in the school canteen.

(A) Right   B Wrong   C Doesn't Say

31   David likes stamp collecting and chess.

A   Right   B Wrong   (C) Doesn't Say

32   David will tell Juan about his hobbies the next time he writes.

(A) Right   B Wrong   C Doesn't Say

Part 5
Questions 33 – 40

Read the article about life in England.
Choose the best word (A, B or C) for each space (33 – 40).
For questions 33 – 40, mark A, B or C.

•••••• LIFE IN ENGLAND ••••••

In Britain most children start nursery school when they are 3 years <u>0</u>.
After this they begin primary school which they go to <u>33</u> they are 11.
Children <u>34</u> go to State primary schools then usually go to secondary
schools. You must stay <u>35</u> school until you are 16 when you do some
important exams, called GCSE's.

If you do well in <u>36</u> exams you <u>37</u> continue for another 2 years specialis-
ing in three or four <u>38</u>. For example, English, French and German <u>39</u>
Maths, Physics and Chemistry. Then you do more exams called A
Levels and if your <u>40</u> are good you can go to University.

EXAMPLE			ANSWER
0 A old	B young	C age	A

33	A from	B since	Ⓒ until
34	A which	Ⓑ who	C what
35	Ⓐ at	B on	C into
36	Ⓐ these	B this	C that
37	A can't	Ⓑ can	C have
38	A themes	B materials	Ⓒ subjects
39	A and	Ⓑ or	C with
40	Ⓐ marks	B notes	C figures

Part 6
Questions 41 – 50

Complete these letters.
Write one word for each space (41 – 50).

Dear Mr Cooper,

I (Example: **am**) sorry I cannot come __41__ class today. I __42__
to stay __43__ home for a week because I have got the flu. I
hope to be back at school on Monday.
__44__ you send me __45__ homework, please?.

Yours,

Sarah

Dear Sarah,

Thank you for __46__ note. I hope you get better __47__ .
If you want to do some exercises you can __48__ the one in
your book __49__ page nine.
I hope to see you in class __50__ week.
Yours,
Mr Cooper

Key

41 to   42 have   43 at   44 Can/Could   45 some
46 your   47 soon   48 do   49 on   50 next

Mark Smith wants to go on the school trip.
Read this information about him and then fill in the form the school gave him.

> **Mark Smith is 14 years old. He was born on the second of March 1979. He's in class nine. He has some problems with asthma and he is allergic to dust.**

APPLICATION FORM

First Name:		Mark
Surname:	51	Smith
Date of Birth:	52	2 March 1979
Class:	53	Nine
Any Health Problems:	54	Asthma
Any Allergies:	55	Dust

Part 8
Question 56

You will be late home from school today. Your mother is at work.
Write a note to her.

Say:

    <u>why</u> you will be late.
    <u>what</u> you will be doing and <u>when</u> you will be home.

Write 20 – 25 words.

LISTENING PAPER

Part 1
Questions 1 – 5

Listen to the tape
You will hear five short conversations.
You will hear each conversation twice.
There is one question for each conversation.
For questions 1 – 5, put a tick ✓ under the right answer.

Here is an example:

EXAMPLE

0   Which class do they have to go to?

2B   **2V**   **2P**

A ✓   B ☐   C ☐

---

1   What time does the Spanish class begin?

9.15   **9.45**   **8.15**

A ✓   B ☐   C ☐

2   How long does the class last?

One hour   **3/4 hour**   **1 hour 1/4**

A ☐   B ✓   C ☐

3   When is the Spanish exam?

5th March   **15th March**   **5th May**

A ✓   B ☐   C ☐

4   Which page does the teacher say?

150   **130**   **113**

A ☐   B ✓   C ☐

5   Where does the teacher ask John to go?

To the teachers   **To the room**   **To the teachers'
                                                    room**

A ☐   B ☐   C ✓

TAPESCRIPT

Listen to the instructions for Part One.

You will hear five short conversations.
You will hear each conversation twice.
There is one question for each conversation.
For questions 1 – 5, put a tick ✓ under the right answer.

Here is an example:

Example: Which class do they have to go to?

Excuse me, which class do we have to go to?
Class 2B
Thanks
Not at all
The answer is 2B, so there is a tick in box A.
Now we are ready to start.
Look at question one.

One. what time does the Spanish class begin?
When is the Spanish class?
At a quarter past nine
I thought it was at 8.15, are you sure?
Yes, of course.

Now listen again.

Two. How long does the class last?
What time does the class finish?
At 10 or 10.15. Let's look at the timetable.
It says at 10 o'clock and it starts at 9.15, remember.
Oh good, it's not a one hour class.

Now listen again.

Three. When is the Spanish exam?
Will we have an exam this term?
Yes, but not until March.
What date exactly?
The fifth of March.

Now listen again.

Four. Which page does the teacher say?
Can you open your books please?
What page?
Page one hundred and thirty.
Thanks.

Now listen again.

Five. Where does the teacher ask John to go?
John, can you get me everybody's notebooks please?
From the teachers' room?
That's right.
OK.

Now listen again.

This is the end of Part One.

TAPESCRIPT

Now look at Part Two.

Listen to Tim phoning Lucy about their homework.
Tim asks Lucy six questions.
What does he ask Lucy about each subject?

For questions 6-10, write a letter (A-H) next to each subject.
You will hear the conversation twice.

Lucy: Hello

Tim: Hello Lucy, it's me,Tim. Can you tell me what page the latin homework is on?

Lucy: Just a moment I'll get my notebook. It's on page 67.

Tim: What units must we study for biology?

Lucy: Units 5 and 6.

Tim: And what exercises do we have to do for mathematics?

Lucy: Exercises 3 and 4.

Tim: What's the title of the English composition?

Lucy: "The Happiest Day of my Life".

Tim: Next question. What chapters do we have to study for History?

Lucy: Chapters 3 and 4. Tim, you're asking a lot of questions.

Tim: I know. I'm sorry but I left my notebook at school.This is the last question! What vocabulary do we have to study for French?

Lucy: The vocabulary of Units 1 and 2.

Tim: Lucy?

Lucy: Yes?

Tim: I don't think today is going to be the happiest day of my life!

Now listen again.

This is the end of Part Two.

Part 2
Questions 6 – 10

Listen to Tim phoning Lucy to ask about their homework.
Tim asked Lucy six questions.
What did he ask Lucy about each subject?

For questions 6 – 10, write a letter (A – H) next to each subject.
You will hear the conversation twice.

EXAMPLE	ANSWER
0 Latin	B

SUBJECT		QUESTION
6 Biology	☐	A What exercises?
		B What page?
7 Maths	☐	C What number?
8 English	☐	D What chapters?
		E Title of composition
9 History	☐	F What units?
10 French	☐	G What vocabulary?
		H What notebook?

Key

6 F   **7** A   **8** E   **9** D   **10** G

Part 3
Questions 11 – 15

Listen to Jane telling Toby what happened in Latin class.

For questions 11 – 15 tick ✓ A, B or C.
You will hear the conversation twice.

EXAMPLE		ANSWER	
0 Mike arrived late for	A	school.	
	B	today.	
	C	Latin class.	✓

11	Mr Spencer sent Mike	A	out.	
		B	home.	✓
		C	away.	

12	Mike said	A	he was late.	
		B	he was sorry.	✓
		C	he was on time.	

13	Mike's father is	A	away.	✓
		B	at home.	
		C	out.	

14	Mr Spencer never listens to	A	students.	
		B	pupils.	
		C	excuses.	✓

15	Jane will speak to Mr Spencer	A	at lunch time.	
		B	at break time.	✓
		C	in the class.	

TAPESCRIPT

Now look at Part Three.

Listen to Jane talking to Toby about what happened in her Latin class.

For questions 11 – 15, tick ✓ A, B or C.
You will hear the conversation twice.

Look at questions 11 – 15 now. You have twenty seconds.

Now listen to the conversation.

Jane: Hi Toby

Toby: Hi

Jane: Do you know what happened in my Latin class today?

Toby: Mike arrived late again, I suppose.

Jane: Yes, but this time Mr Spencer sent him home.

Toby: What?

Jane: Yes he told him he wanted to teach him a lesson.

Toby: Did he say sorry for arriving late?

Jane: Yes, but Mr Spencer said it was easy to say sorry but not so easy to be punctual!

Toby: What will his parents say?

Jane: I don't know. His father is away on a business trip. He is away a lot. Mike has a new baby brother and he has to help his mother in the morning.

Toby: Mr Spencer doesn't know that.

Jane: No, but that is because he never listens to excuses.

Toby: Why don't you speak to Mr Spencer. You are the class representative.

Jane: That's a good idea, I'll speak to him tomorrow at break time.

Now listen again.

This is the end of Part Three.

TAPESCRIPT

Now look at Part Four.

You will hear a girl speaking on the telephone.
She wants to speak to Brian but he is not there.

Listen and complete questions 16-20.
You will hear the conversation twice.

M   602819

F   Hello, could I speak to Brian please?

M   I'm sorry Brian's not in at the moment. Can I take a message?

F   Yes, please.

M   Just hold on a minute until I get a pen. OK. What's your name?

F   My name's Jenny Gowdy.

M   Sorry, how do you spell your surname?

F   G O W D Y

M   G O W D Y

F   That's right. Could you ask him to come to my house at 6 o'clock this evening.

M   Yes, of course. Anything else?

F   Yes, I nearly forgot. Could you ask him to bring his history book. That's the most important thing because we have an exam tomorrow.

M   Don't worry I'll tell him and good luck with the exam. I hope you both pass.

F   Thanks a lot. Oh, one more thing, my Mum says he must stay for dinner.

M   That's fine. I'll tell him everything. Bye.

F   Bye and thanks again.

Now listen again.

This is the end of Part Four.

Part 4
Questions 16 – 20

Listen to a girl speaking on the telephone.
She wants to speak to Brian but he is not there.

For questions 16 – 20, complete the message to Brian.
You will hear the conversation twice.

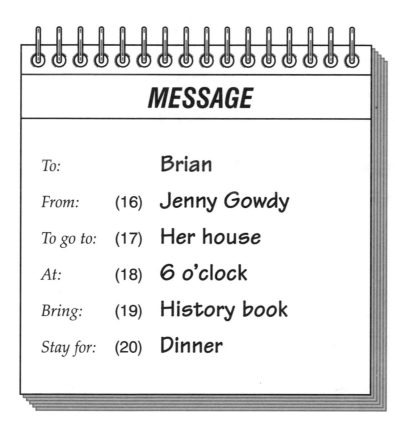

MESSAGE

To:		Brian
From:	(16)	Jenny Gowdy
To go to:	(17)	Her house
At:	(18)	6 o'clock
Bring:	(19)	History book
Stay for:	(20)	Dinner

Listen to some information about a school.
For questions 21 – 25, complete the information about the school.
You will hear the conversation twice.

LITTLEFIELD SCHOOL

Closed until:		16 August
Office open from:	(21)	Monday 16 August
In the morning to	(22)	1 o'clock
Tuesday 17th meeting for:	(23)	Students who did A levels
Thursday for:	(24)	Students who did A levels and their parents
New pupils have to come on:	(25)	Friday 20th August at 8 o'clock

TAPESCRIPT

Now look at Part Five

You will hear some information about a school.
Listen and complete questions 21 – 25.
You will hear the information twice.

Thank you for calling Littlefield School. This is a recorded message.

The school is closed for the summer holidays from August 1st - 15th. The office will be open again on Monday, 16th August. The office is open from 9.00 in the morning until 1.00 and from 3 o'clock to 5 o'clock in the afternoon.

Students who did A'Levels have to come to see their teachers at 9 o'clock in the morning on Tuesday 17th August. They have to come again on Thursday at 9 o'clock in the evening with their parents.

New pupils have to come with their parents to meet the teachers and see the school on Friday 20th August at 8 o'clock in the evening.

If you have any questions, please leave a message with your name and telephone number and we will ring you as soon as possible.

Thank you for calling.

Now listen again.

This is the end of Part Five.

TEST 3 HOME TOWN

READING AND WRITING PAPER

Part 1
Questions 1 – 5

Who are these notices for?
For questions 1 – 5, mark A, B or C.

EXAMPLE		ANSWER
0 **NO STOPPING**	A people B pedestrians C drivers	C

1 NO PARKING

(A) drivers

B pedestrians

C conductors

2 **CITY CENTRE STRAIGHT AHEAD**

A campers

(B) drivers

C shop assistants

3 *CAR PARK FULL*

A children

(B) car owners

C runners

4 **DON'T CROSS**

A lorry drivers

B drivers

(C) pedestrians

5 **NO LEFT TURN**

A children

B shoppers

(C) drivers

Questions 6 – 10

Which notice (A – H) says this (6 – 10)?
For questions 6 – 10, mark the correct letter (A – H).

EXAMPLE	ANSWER
0 You can buy stamps here	G

6   If you need urgent treatment go here.

7   You can ask for a map of the town here.

8   You can buy lottery tickets here.

9   We don't close for lunch.

10   If you see an accident go here.

A   **Museum open 9am to 5pm**

B   *LOTTERY TICKETS ON SALE HERE*

C   Tourist Information

D   **EMERGENCIES ONLY**

E   **HOSPITAL ENTRANCE**

F   **Police Station**

G   **Post Office**

H   **WINNING LOTTERY TICKET SOLD HERE**

Key

6 D   7 C   8 B   9 A   10 F

Part 2
Questions 11 – 15

Read the descriptions (11 – 15) of some places.
What is the name of each place (A – H)?
For questions 11 – 15, mark the correct letter (A – H).

EXAMPLE	ANSWER
0 You can buy food here.	F

11   You can get tourist
        information here.

12   You can study here when
        you are eighteen.

13   You can buy nearly
        everything here.

14   If you want to borrow books,
        you go here.

15   You can see interesting
        old things here.

PLACES

A   shopping centre

B   museum

C   university

D   town hall

E   bookshop

F   supermarket

G   library

H   secondary school

Key

11 D   **12** C   **13** A   **14** G   **15** B

Part 3
Questions 16 – 20

Complete the five conversations.
For questions 16 – 20, mark A, B or C.

EXAMPLE		ANSWER
0 Do you need any stamps?	A Yes, I have. B Yes, I do. C No, I needn't.	B

16   What time does the museum open?

A   Since 9 o'clock.
B   At 9 o'clock.
C   9 hours.

17   Where is the nearest church?

A   Yes, of course.
B   Two hours.
C   I don't know.

18   Are there many Chinese restaurants in Oxford?

A   Yes, much.
B   Yes, a lot.
C   Yes, a little.

19   What is Oxford most famous for?

A   His boat race.
B   Her street.
C   Its university.

20   Is it far to the town centre?

A   Not very.
B   A lot.
C   Far away.

Questions 21 – 25

Complete the conversation?
What does Jenny say to Mary?
For questions 21 – 25, mark the correct letter (A – H).

EXAMPLE		ANSWER
Jenny:	Can you answer some questions about Oxford University?	D
Mary	0............	

Jenny: How old is Oxford university?

Mary: 21 **H**

Jenny: How many colleges has it got?

Mary: 22 **C**

Jenny: Can anyone go to it?

Mary: 23 **F**

Jenny: How long do you have to study to get your degree?

Mary: 24 **B**

Jenny: It's a beautiful university. I would love to go there.

Mary: 25 **E**

Jenny: Because I don't think I'm intelligent enough!

A   It depends on your notes.

B   3 or 4 years.

C   I don't know.

D   Yes, of course I can.

E   Why don't you?

F   Yes, if they get excellent marks.

G   It's beautiful, isn't it?

H   About 800 years old.

Part 4
Questions 26 – 32

Read the article about a girl from Barcelona.
Are sentences 26 – 32 'Right' (A) or 'Wrong' (B).

If there is not enough information to answer 'Right' (A) or 'Wrong' (B), choose 'Doesn't say' (C).

For questions 26 – 32, mark A, B or C.

I LOVE ENGLISH!

Yolanda Pérez is just 15 years old. This summer she is studying English in Oxford. This is what she told our interviewer.

What do you think of Oxford?

Well, I think it's fantastic. There are many beautiful buildings, the parks, the river, the university...

Is there anything else you especially like about it?

Yes, the wonderful atmosphere in the streets with so many tourists and students from all over the world. There are also lots of interesting museums to visit and plenty of sports facilities.

What do you not like about Oxford?

Most people say the weather but because I am only here for July and August I don't mind a little rain and some cloudy days. In my country it's too hot in August.

Where are you staying in Oxford?

I'm staying with a very nice family. I must say the food is much nicer than I thought it would be.

Do you like learning English?

I love learning English. I want to be an English teacher when I am older. But now I must go - my next class starts in five minutes.

EXAMPLE	ANSWER
0 Yolanda think Oxford is wonderful.	A
A Right B Wrong C Doesn't say	

26 Yolanda likes the atmosphere in Oxford.

(A) Right B Wrong C Doesn't say

27 There are few sports facilities.

A Right (B) Wrong C Doesn't say

28 Yolanda thought the food would be better.

A Right (B) Wrong C Doesn't say

29 Yolanda likes pubs a lot.

A Right B Wrong (C) Doesn't say

30 Yolanda doesn't mind the English climate in summer.

(A) Right B Wrong C Doesn't say

31 Yolanda is an English teacher.

A Right (B) Wrong C Doesn't say

32 Her next class begins soon.

(A) Right B Wrong C Doesn't say

Part 5
Questions 33 – 40

Read the article about an English town.
Choose the best word (A, B or C) for each space (33 – 40).

> ····· **AN ENGLISH TOWN** ·····
>
> In an English town or village most people live in houses ___0___ a garden. The average family ___33___ got two children and the mother and father usually ___34___ work. A lot of families ___35___ have a cat or a dog. The town usually has post offices, schools, banks, churches, cinemas, restaurants, discos, pubs etc. It also ___36___ a police station, a town hall and a hospital.
>
> English pubs are ___37___ all over the world. They are not just ___38___ because you can eat in them, play snooker or darts, listen to music and so on. In short, you ___39___ have a very good ___40___ there.

EXAMPLE						ANSWER
0 A in	B	with	C	from		B

33 (A) has   B   is   C   are

34 A   two   (B) both   C   the two

35 (A) also   B   too   C   to

36 A   does   (B) has   C   is

37 A   visit   (B) famous   C   in

38 (A) bars   B   a drink   C   for drink

39 A   do   (B) can   C   have

40 A   funny   B   enjoy   (C) time

Part 6
Questions 41 – 50

Complete these letters.
Write one word for each space (41 – 50).

Dear Nigel,

We're having a scout meeting (Example: **in**) the church hall
___41___ afternoon.   It will begin ___42___ four o'clock and
___43___ about seven o'clock.   If you ___44___ come please
leave a message for me.

See you ___45___.

Yours,

John Smith

Dear Scout Master,

Thank ___46___ for your note.   I am very ___47___ but I can't
___48___ to the meeting this afternoon.   I have a very difficult
exam ___49___ Monday morning and my mother says I
___50___ to study.

I'll see you at church tomorrow.

Yours

Nigel Brown

Key

41 this   **42** at   **43** finish/end   **44** can   **45** soon/later
46 you   **47** sorry   **48** come   **49** on   **50** have

Part 7
Questions 51 – 55

Read the information about a family who want to vote.
Fill in the information on the census card.

Jonathan Cowling is from London. He's nearly 39.
He's single and he lives at 266, St Margaret's Road,
Twickenham, London.

CENSUS CARD

First Name:		Jonathan
Surname:	51	Cowling
Sex:	52	Male
Age:	53	38
Full address:	54	266 St Margaret's Road, Twickenham
Marital status: (single/married)	55	Single

Part 8
Question 56

You want to go to the cinema with a friend. Leave a note for him.

Say:

    <u>what</u> film you want to see.

    <u>where</u> and <u>when</u> to meet you.

Write 20 – 25 words.

LISTENING PAPER

Part 1
Questions 1 – 5

Listen to the tape.
You will hear five short conversations.
You will hear each conversation twice.
There is one question for each conversation.
For questions 1 – 5, put a tick ✓ under the right answer.

Here is an example:

EXAMPLE

0 What time does the post office open?

0830	**0900**	**0930**
A ☐	B ☐	C ✓

---

1 How much does a lottery ticket cost?

£1.50	**£1.00**	**£1.15**
A ☐	B ☐	C ✓

2 When is the film on?

Tuesday 4th	Thursday 14th	Tuesday 14th
A ✓	B ☐	C ☐

3 Where is the police station?

Behind the town hall	**Next to the town hall**	**Opposite the town hall**
A ☐	B ✓	C ☐

4 How many books can the man borrow from the library?

3 times a week	3 every 2 weeks	2 every 3 weeks
A ☐	B ✓	C ☐

5 Which church does the girl go to?

St Mary's	St Paul's	Opposite St Paul's
A ☐	B ✓	C ☐

TAPESCRIPT

Look at the instructions for Part One.

You will hear five short conversations.
You will hear each conversation twice.
There is one question for each conversation.
For questions 1-5, put a tick under the right answer.

Here is an example:

Example: What time does the post office open?
F   Excuse me, do you know what time the post office opens?
M   At half past nine, I think
F   Thank you
M   You're welcome
The answer is half past nine so there is a tick in box C.
Now we are ready to start.
Look at question one.

One. How much does a lottery ticket cost?
M   How much arc lottery tickets?
F   £1.15p each. Do you want one?
M   Yes please.
F   Here you are and here's your change.
M   Thank you.

Now listen again.

Two. When is the film on?
F   Let's go to see 4 Weddings and a Funeral.
M   When's it on?
F   Next Tuesday, Tuesday the 4th.
M   OK. That sounds great.

Now listen again.

Three. Where is the police station?
F   Can you tell me where the police station is please?
M   Certainly. It's very near. It's over there, beside the town hall.
F   Thanks a lot.
M   Not at all.

Now listen again.

Four. How many books can the man borrow from the library?
M   May I borrow four books?
F   No, I'm sorry, you can only take three.
M   Do I have to return them in a week?
F   No, you can borrow them for two weeks.
M   All right, that's fine.

Now listen again.

Five. Which church does the girl go to?
M   Do you go to church on Sundays?
F   Yes, I go to St Paul's.
M   Where's that?
F   It's opposite St Mary's School.

Now listen again.

This is the end of Part One.

TAPESCRIPT

Now look at Part Two.

Listen to Lucy talking to Rachel about her shopping trip.
Lucy went to six shops
What did she buy in each shop.

For questions 6-10, write a letter (A-H) next to each shop.
You will hear the conversation twice.

Rachel: What did you do today Lucy?

Lucy: I spent all day shopping. First I went to the supermarket to get the groceries. Then I went to the off licence to get some champagne.

Rachel: Where did you do your shopping?

Lucy: In the new shopping centre. That's why I spent so long.

Rachel: Did you buy any clothes in the shopping centre?

Lucy: Yes, I bought a lovely red dress in the boutique. I nearly bought a pair of jeans too but they were too expensive.

Rachel: There's a garden centre there too, isn't there?

Lucy: Yes, I got a beautiful plant there for my mother for Mother's Day. She really prefers flowers but my brother is buying her some.

Rachel: Did you get anything else?

Lucy: I'm afraid I did. I bought a compact disc for myself in the record shop. Oh, and a little doll for my neighbour's new baby in the toy shop.

Rachel: You certainly bought a lot. I hope you have enough money left to come out with me tonight!

Now listen again.

This is the end of Part Two.

Part 2
Questions 6 – 10

Listen to Lucy talking to Rachel about her shopping trip.
Lucy went to six shops.
What did she buy in each shop?

For questions 6 – 10, write a letter (A – H) next to each shop.
You will hear the conversation twice.

EXAMPLE	ANSWER
0 Supermarket	B

	SHOP			**THINGS BOUGHT**	
6	Off licence	☐		A	Champagne
				B	Groceries
7	Boutique	☐		C	Jeans
8	Garden centre	☐		D	Dress
				E	Plant
9	Record shop	☐		F	Flowers
				G	Doll
10	Toy shop	☐		H	Compact disc

Key

6 A   7 D   8 E   9 H   10 G

Part 3
Questions 11 – 15

Listen to David talking to the hospital receptionist and then to his friend Michael.
For questions 11 – 15, tick ☑ A, B or C.
You will hear the conversation twice.

EXAMPLE	ANSWER	
0 The patient's name is	A Michael Curran.	☑
	B Michael Curren.	☐
	C Michael Currin.	☐

11	Michael is on	A the second floor.	☑
		B the second ward.	☐
		C the men's floor.	☐
12	Michael broke his leg playing	A basketball.	☐
		B American football.	☐
		C football.	☑
13	Michael will be in hospital for	A two weeks.	☑
		B two months	☐
		C two days.	☐
14	The nurses are	A not so bad.	☐
		B not very good.	☐
		C very nice.	☑
15	David is going to bring him	A some biscuits and a drink.	☐
		B fruit and biscuits.	☑
		C Some fruit and a cake.	☐

TAPESCRIPT

Now look at Part Three.

Listen to David talking to the hospital receptionist and then to his friend Michael.

For questions 11 – 15, tick ☑ A, B or C.
You will hear the conversations twice.

Look at questions 11 – 15 now. You have twenty seconds.
Now listen to the conversations.

Receptionist:	Good afternoon, can I help you?
David:	Yes, I'd like to see a patient please.
Receptionist:	What's his name?
David:	Michael Curran.
Receptionist:	Could you spell his surname please?
David:	Yes, of course, it's C U R R A N.
Receptionist:	Oh yes, he's on the second floor in the men's ward.
David:	Thanks.
Receptionist:	You're welcome.
	**********************************
David:	I Ii, Mike.
Michael:	Hello David. It's great to see you.
David:	How's your leg?
Michael:	It's broken. I broke it five minutes before the end of the match and now I can't play football for two months.
David:	That's really bad luck. How long will you be in hospital for?
Michael:	For two weeks, but it's not so bad, the nurses are very kind.
David:	What's the food like?
Michael:	Not very good. It's just like school food.
David:	I'll bring you some biscuits and fruit tomorrow.
Michael:	Thanks a lot, Dave.

Now listen again.

TAPESCRIPT

Now look at Part Four.

You will hear a girl called Susanna reporting a robbery to the police.

Listen and complete questions 16-20.
You will hear the conversation twice.

Policeman: Good morning, can I help you?

Girl: I hope so. My handbag was stolen this afternoon at about 4 o'clock.

Policeman: Oh dear! I'm sorry to hear that. Can you tell me your name and surname.

Girl: Yes it's Susanna, Susanna Peters, that's P E T E R S.

Policeman: Where did it happen?

Girl: In a shop. Marks & Spencers. I was looking at the jumpers. I put my hand-bag down for a moment and when I turned round it wasn't there.

Policeman: Did you see anyone with it?

Girl: No, but I saw a girl and a boy running away very quickly. He was short, blond and fat and she was tall with long, red hair.

Policeman: Did you see their faces?

Girl: No, I didn't

Policeman: What was in your handbag?

Girl: The usual things, make-up, my purse but not a lot of money, photographs .....

Policeman: Ok, Miss Peters, we'll do our best to find your handbag.

Now listen again.

This is the end of Part Four.

Listen to a girl called Susanna reporting a robbery to the police.

For questions 16 – 20, fill in the crime report.
You will hear the conversation twice.

CRIME REPORT

Name:		Susanna
Surname:	(16)	Peters
Robbed at:	(17)	About 4 o'clock
in:	(18)	In a shop/Marks & Spencer's
by:	(19)	A girl and a boy
Handbag contained purse, make-up and:	(20)	Photographs

Listen to some information about a Science Museum.

For questions 21 – 25, complete the information about the Science Museum.
You will hear the message twice.

SCIENCE MUSEUM

Opens:		9.00am
Closes:	(21)	6 o'clock
Cost for adults:	(22)	£1.60
For students and children:	(23)	80p
Special school trips on:	(24)	Wednesdays
Creche for children under:	(25)	5

TAPESCRIPT

Now look at Part Five.

You will hear some information about a Science Museum.
Listen and complete questions 21 – 25.

You will hear the information twice.

Thank you for calling the Science Museum. This is a recorded message.

The Science Museum is open from nine o'clock in the morning until six o'clock in the evening. Last entrance is at five o'clock. It costs one pound sixty to enter the museum, but only 80 pence for students and children.

The museum is closed to the public on Wednesdays. Special school trips, or other groups, can be arranged with a guide.   This is possible only on Wednesdays, and you must write at least two weeks before you want to come. Telephone bookings are not accepted.

Children under twelve must be accompanied by an adult. We have a creche where young children under five can be left but parents must return to see their children every half an hour.

There is also a cafe on the top floor which is open the same hours as the museum.

Thank you for calling and we look forward to seeing you at the Science Museum.

Now listen again.

This is the end of Part Five.

TEST 4   HOBBIES AND SPORTS

READING AND WRITING PAPER

Part 1
Questions 1 – 5

Who are these notices for?
For questions 1 – 5, mark A, B or C.

EXAMPLE		ANSWER
0 **You must change your shoes**	A people entering a gym B people playing table-tennis C people playing billiards	A

1   **Please return balls**

(A)   tennis players

B   swimmers

C   chess players

2   **YOU MUST WEAR A BATHING CAP**

A   golfers

(B)   swimmers

C   basketball players

3   **QUIET PLEASE**

A   football spectators

B   rugby spectators

(C)   tennis spectators

4   **MEMBERS ONLY**

A   people joining a club

B   people leaving a club

(C)   people entering a club

5   **Family changing rooms**

A   families who want to change rooms

B   people who want to change families

(C)   families who want to change together

Questions 6 – 10

Which notice (A – H) says this (6 – 10)?
For questions 6 – 10, mark the correct letter (A – H).

EXAMPLE	ANSWER
0 You can learn to dance in the afternoon	C

6   You can shop in a new sports shop soon.

7   Skis are cheaper now.

8   Our shop is open this afternoon.

9   If you want to go to the big match, come in!

10   At the moment all our products are cheaper.

A   **FOOTBALL TICKETS ON SALE HERE**

B   **BIG REDUCTIONS ON SKIS**

C   **BALLET CLASSES 3–6PM**

D   **CHEAPEST SPORTS SHOP IN TOWN**

E   **SKIS FOR HIRE**

F   **EVERYTHING REDUCED**

G   **SPORTS SHOP OPENING SOON**

H   **CLOSED FOR LUNCH 1–2 PM**

Key

6 G   7 B   8 H   9 A   10 F

Part 2
Questions 11 – 15

Read the descriptions (11 – 15) of some places.
What is the name of each place (A – H)?
For questions 11 – 15, mark the correct letter (A – H).

EXAMPLE	ANSWER
0 You can skate here.	B

		PLACES
11	If you play tennis, you book one.	
		A track
12	You play football here.	B ice rink
		C beach
13	If you do athletics, you run here.	D pitch
		E camp
14	This is where you go to collect shells.	F gym
		G court
15	You do exercises to get fit here.	H race course

Key

11 G   **12** D   **13** A   **14** C   **15** F

Part 3
Questions 16 – 20

Complete the five conversations.
For questions 16 – 20, mark A, B or C.

EXAMPLE		ANSWER
0 Do you like acting?	A Yes, I have. B No, I'm not. C Yes, I do.	C

16   Can you ride a horse?

(A) Yes, I can.
B   No, I don't.
C   Yes, I do.

17   Do you want to come cycling with me on Saturday?

(A) Yes, please.
B   On Saturday.
C   Yes, I went.

18   How much do the tickets for the football match cost?

A   Very much.
B   That's expensive.
(C) I don't know.

19   Are you playing hockey on Sunday?

A   That's all right.
(B) I hope so.
C   I think I have.

20   When is the rugby match?

A   In the rugby club.
B   Last week.
(C) On Saturday.

Questions 21 – 25

Complete the conversation.
What does Richard say to Christian?
For questions 21 – 25, mark the correct letter (A – H).

EXAMPLE	ANSWER
Christian: Hi Richard, how are things?	B
Richard: 0............	

Christian:	Fine. are you playing basketball on Saturday?	A	No, it's an away match.
		B	OK, what about you?
Richard:	21 **E**	C	Please don't be late.
Christian:	I'd like to go to watch you play with a friend	D	The bus leaves at 6 in the morning.
		E	Yes, of course I am.
Richard:	22 **F**	F	That would be great.
Christian:	Where is the match? Is it at home?	G	The bus leaves at 3 in the afternoon.
Richard:	23 **A**	H	Please come early.
Christian:	What time do we have to leave?		
Richard:	24 **D**		
Christian:	That's very early. I'll have to go to bed early tonight.		
Richard:	25 **C**		
Christian:	Don't worry. I won't.		

Part 4
Questions 26 – 32

Read the interview with a British P.E. teacher called Mr Brown.
Are sentences 26 – 32 'Right' (A) or 'Wrong' (B)?

If there is not enough information to answer 'Right' (A) or 'Wrong' (B),
choose 'Doesn't say' (C).

For questions 26 – 32, mark A, B or C.

What sports do you play at your school?
In winter we play rugby or football or go cross-country running. Some girls play netball or hockey and next year we hope to have a boy's hockey team too.

Do only boys play rugby or football?
No, we have a very good girls' football team and we've just started a girls' rugby team.

Is sport compulsory in British schools?
Yes, you have to play sport at least one afternoon a week, but you don't have to take a sports exam, as you do in some countries for example, Spain.

What sports do you play in summer?
The boys play cricket but I'm sure it won't be long until the girls play too. Boys and girls go swimming, do athletics and girls play rounders which is similar to baseball. We also have tennis courts.

Is sport a popular subject?
Yes, very. Much more than before because everyone is health conscious now and wants to get fit. The only thing I don't like about being a sports teacher is that the younger children never want to have a shower!

26 Only boys play rugby at Mr Brown's school.

A   Right   (B) Wrong   C   Doesn't say

27 Some boys play hockey.

A   Right   (B) Wrong   C   Doesn't say

28 The girls' rugby team is very good.

A   Right   B   Wrong   (C) Doesn't say

29 Sport is compulsory in British schools.

(A) Right   B   Wrong   C   Doesn't say

30 The pupils have to do a sports exam.

A   Right   (B) Wrong   C   Doesn't say

31 There is a girls' cricket team.

A   Right   (B) Wrong   C   Doesn't say

32 The younger children don't like having a shower.

(A) Right   B   Wrong   C   Doesn't say

Part 5
Questions 33 – 40

Read the article about cricket.
Choose the best word (A, B or C) for each space (33 – 40).
For questions 33 – 40, mark A, B or C.

═══ CRICKET ═══

Most people know there is a sport called cricket __0__ they don't understand how it is played.   This is not surprising! Cricket is a very complicated sport.

There are eleven __33__ on each team and they all __34__ white clothes. They play with two bats and a ball.   One of the strangest things __35__ cricket is that the match can go on all day or __36__ for five days! It is played in summer in England and it is a very typical sight to see families in pretty villages __37__ cricket played __38__ grass.

Cricket began in England but it is also very popular __39__ India, Pakistan, the West Indies, Australia and New Zealand.

People get very passionate about cricket in __40__ countries but the rest of the world thinks it's very boring!

EXAMPLE			ANSWER
0 A but	B and	C or	A

33 (A) players   B   games   C   teams

34   A   dress   B   carry   (C) wear

35 (A) about   B   on   C   over

36   A   during   (B) even   C   including

37 (A) watching   B   looking   C   watching at

38   A   over   (B) on   C   above

39   A   at   (B) in   C   into

40   A   this   B   that   (C) these

Part 6
Questions 41 – 50

Complete these letters.
Write one word for each space (41 – 50).

Dear Min,

I (Example: **am**) sorry I can't wait ___41___ you any longer.
I ___42___ to go to the doctor. If you ___43___ I can play tennis
with you tomorrow ___44___.

___45___ you book the court?

Thanks,

Mary

Dear Mary,

I'm ___46___ I arrived late yesterday. I have booked ___47___
court for 3 o'clock. Is that ___48___? Can you bring an extra
racket ___49___ mine is broken?

See you ___50___.

Min

Key

41 for   42 have   43 wish/want/like

44 morning/afternoon/evening   45 Can   46 sorry

47 a/the   48 OK/alright   49 because   50 then/tomorrow

Part 7
Questions 51 – 55

Read this information about a family who want to join a sports club.
Fill in the information on the application form.

Mr and Mrs Richardson have got two daughters and one
son. Mr and Mrs Richardson both play squash and tennis.
Their son likes table-tennis and swimming but their
daughters don't like either tennis or swimming, they prefer
gymnastics.

FAMILY APPLICATION FORM

Surname: Richardson

Number of children:

51	3

Sports they are interested in:

Mr Richardson

52	Squash/tennis

Mrs Richardson

53	Squash/tennis

Their son:

54	Table-tennis/ swimming

Their daughters:

55	Gymnastics

Part 8
Question 56

You want to go cycling with your friend, David, tomorrow morning.

Write a note to David.

Say:

where to meet you and at what time.

Also what he has to bring.

Write 20 – 25 words.

LISTENING PAPER

Part 1
Questions 1 – 5

Listen to the tape.
You will hear five short conversations.
You will hear each conversation twice.
There is one question for each conversation.
For questions 1 – 5, put a tick ✓ under the right answer.

Here is an example:

EXAMPLE

0 Which hockey stick does the boy want?

The red one   **The blue one**   **The red and blue one**

A ✓   B ☐   C ☐

---

1   What sports does the woman play?

golf and table-tennis   table-tennis   **tennis and golf**

A ☐   B ☐   C ✓

2   How much does the court cost per hour?

£1.30   **£1.50**   **£1.15**

A ☐   B ✓   C ☐

3   When is the handball match?

5th July   **6th July**   **4th July**

A ✓   B ☐   C ☐

4   Where is the squash club?

on the right   **on the left**   **in the centre**

A ☐   B ✓   C ☐

5   What time does the match begin?

3.30   **4.30**   **3.13**

A ✓   B ☐   C ☐

TAPESCRIPT

Test Four

Look at the instructions for Part One.

You will hear five short conversations.

You will hear each conversation twice.

There is one question for each conversation.

For questions 1-5, put a tick under the right answer.

Here is an example:

Example: Which hockey stick does the boy want?
F   Can I help you?
M   Yes, please. I'd like one of these hockey sticks.
F   Do you prefer the blue one or the red one?
M   I'd rather have the red one.
The answer is the red one, so there is a tick in box A.
Now we are ready to start. Look at question one.

One. What sports does the woman play?
F1   Do you play any sports?
F2   Yes, I do.
F1   What do you play?
F2   I play golf and tennis.

Now listen again.

Two. How much does the court cost per hour?
M   I'd like to book a court please.
F   Certainly. For what time?
M   For eleven. How much does it cost?
F   £1.50 an hour.
M   That's fine.

Now listen again.

Three. When is the handball match?
F   Are you going to the handball match?
M   I'd like to. When is it?
F   It's on the 5th of July, at 4 o'clock.
M   I'm going to a concert later that day, at six, but I'll try to go.

Now listen again.

Four. Where is the squash club?
M   Excuse me, can you tell me where the squash club is?
F   Of course, go straight down this road and it's on your left.
M   Thanks very much.
F   Not at all.

Now listen again.

Five. What time does the match begin?
M   What time does the match begin?
M   I'm not sure. Let's look in the newspaper.
M   Good idea.
M   Yes, here it is. It starts at 3.30.

Now listen again.

This is the end of Part One

TAPESCRIPT

Now look at Part Two.

Listen to William talking to Raymond about summer camp.
Here are six of the sports you can play.
What does the camp provide for each of these sports?

For questions 6 – 10, write a letter (A – H) next to each sport.
You will hear the conversation twice.

William: Guess what? I'm going to summer camp in July.

Raymond: You're lucky! I'd love to go.

William: It isn't expensive and you can play tennis, squash, hockey, handball, foot-
           ball and things...

Raymond: But I haven't got any racquets or anything.
           ← rackets

William: Don't worry, they have everything: racquets for tennis and squash, hockey
           sticks ...

Raymond: Are there any table-tennis tables? I love table-tennis.

William: Yes, they have bats for table-tennis and for cricket and baseball.   There are
           also nets for handball and volleyball.

Raymond: Have they got horses?

William: Yes, you can go riding and cycling too, they have ordinary bikes and
           mountain bikes.

Raymond: But I suppose you have to pay extra for horse riding?

William: No, you don't.

Raymond: I want to go!

William: Let's ask your parents!
Now listen again.

This is the end of Part Two.

Part 2
Questions 6 – 10

Listen to William talking to Raymond about summer camp.
Here are six of the sports you can play.
What does the camp provide for each of these sports?

For questions 6 – 10, write a letter (A – H) next to each sport.
You will hear the conversation twice.

EXAMPLE	ANSWER
0 Table-tennis	C

SPORT

6   Tennis ☐

7   Hockey ☐

8   Cycling ☐

9   Handball ☐

10   Riding ☐

THINGS BOUGHT

A   Racquet

B   Horse

C   Bat

D   Stick

E   Mountain bikes

F   Motorbike

G   Swimming pool

H   Net

Key

6 A   7 D   8 E   9 H   10 B

Part 3
Questions 11 – 15

Listen to Johnny talking to Paul about rugby.
For questions 11 – 15, tick ✓ A, B or C.
You will hear the conversation twice.

EXAMPLE	ANSWER	
0 The match is	A on the second.	☐
	B on Saturday.	✓
	C in a week.	☐

11 Paul now has to train	A 3 times a week.	✓
	B twice a week.	☐
	C for a week.	☐
12 The trainer is	A nice.	☐
	B friendly.	☐
	C unfriendly.	✓
13 If they win each player will get	A a medal.	☐
	B a cup.	☐
	C a medal and a cup.	✓
14 The match is against	A ANST.	☐
	B ENST.	☐
	C INST.	✓
15 Johnny's going to bring his	A camera.	☐
	B video camera.	✓
	C cassette recorder.	☐

TAPESCRIPT

Now look at Part Three.

Listen to Johnny talking to Paul about rugby.
For questions 11 – 15, tick A, B or C.
You will hear the conversation twice.

Look at Questions 11 – 15 now. You have twenty seconds.

Now listen to the conversation.

Johnny:	Hi Paul, how's the rugby going?
Paul:	Not bad. We're in second position in the league.
Johnny:	That's very good. Are you playing on Saturday?
Paul:	Yes, but it's a cup match. We have to train very hard.
Johnny:	How often do you train?
Paul:	Usually twice a week, but because it's the final we have to train three times now.
Johnny:	What's the trainer like?
Paul:	Well, last year's trainer was really nice, but this one isn't very friendly and he makes us train too much.
Johnny:	What will you get if you win on Saturday?
Paul:	All the players get a medal and also a big cup which everyone can keep in his house for a week. After that it stays in the Club.
Johnny:	Who's the match against?
Paul:	Against a team called Inst.
Johnny:	Called what?
Paul:	Inst. I N S T.
Johnny:	Right, I'll come along. I'll bring my camera. No I won't, I'll bring my father's video camera.
Paul:	Great idea!

Now listen again.

This is the end of Part Three.

TAPESCRIPT

Now look at Part Four

You will hear Charles talking to a friend's sister on the telephone.
He wants to talk to his friend but he is not there.

Listen and complete questions 16 – 20.
You will hear the conversation twice.

M   Hello, can I speak to Matthew please?

F   I'm sorry, he isn't in. This is his sister, Monica.

M   Do you know what time he'll be back?

F   No. I'm afraid I don't but can I take a message?

M   Yes, please but it's a bit complicated and it's very urgent.

F   Don't worry, I'll get a pen ...... Hello.

M   Well, tomorrow's table-tennis match has been changed. It will be at 10 o'clock instead of 11.

F   Ok. I'll tell him. Is there anything else?

M   Yes, we have to meet in front of the cinema and not at the bus station. That's very important. We have to meet at 9.00.

F   All right. He has to be outside the cinema at 9 o'clock and the match is at 10, not 11.

M   That's right. Thanks a lot.

F   Oh, just a minute. Who's speaking please?

M   Sorry, how silly of me. My name's Charles.

F   Bye Charles.

M   Bye.

Now listen again.

This is the end of Part Four.

Part 4
Questions 16 – 20

Listen to Charles talking to a friend's sister on the telephone.
He wants to talk to his friend but he is not there.

For questions 16 – 20, complete the message to Monica's brother.
You will hear the conversation twice.

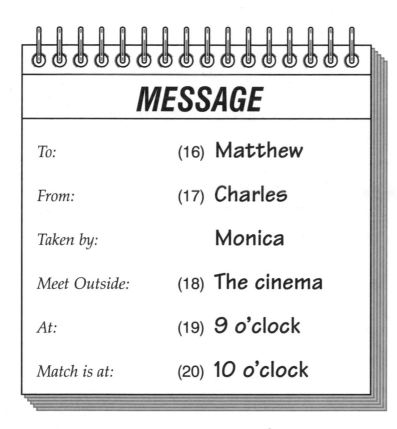

MESSAGE

To:	(16) Matthew
From:	(17) Charles
Taken by:	Monica
Meet Outside:	(18) The cinema
At:	(19) 9 o'clock
Match is at:	(20) 10 o'clock

Part 5
Questions 21 – 25

Listen to some information about a sports club.

For questions 21 – 25, complete the information about the sports club.
You will hear the information twice.

SPORTS CLUB

Opens:		8 o'clock
Closes:	**(21)**	10 o'clock
Membership costs:	**(22)**	£75 a year
Family membership costs:	**(23)**	£200
Price for Children (for One day):		£1
Members can bring one guest per:	**(24)**	day
No visitors on:	**(25)**	Saturday

TAPESCRIPT

Now look at Part Five.

You will hear some information about a sports club.

Listen and complete questions 21 – 25.

You will hear the message twice.

Thank you for calling Windsor Sports Club. This is a recorded message.

The sports club is open every day from eight o'clock in the morning until ten o'clock at night. Last entrance is at nine o'clock. It costs £75 to join the club for one year. Family membership (mother, father and 1, 2 or 3 children) costs £200. There is also a reduction for students.

Non-members can visit the club if they are accompanied by a member. Each member can bring one visitor per day. The cost for the day is £2 for adults, £1.50 for students and £1 for children. You pay the same if you stay one hour or all day. Visitors can come every day except Saturday.

The cafe and bar are open to non-members.

Thank you again for calling.

Now listen again.

This is the end of Part Five.

TEST 5   JOBS

READING AND WRITING PAPER

Part 1
Questions 1 – 5

Who are these notices for?
For questions 1 – 5, mark A, B or C.

EXAMPLE		ANSWER
0 **Change towels every day**	A waitresses B chefs C chambermaids	C

1   **Please type these letters**

(A)   secretaries
B   postmen
C   lawyers

2   **GIVE TABLETS THREE TIMES A DAY**

A   chemists
(B)   nurses
C   patients

3   ALWAYS CHECK CUSTOMERS' CHANGE TWICE

(A)   shop assistants
B   customers
C   clients

4   **Never leave children's classes unattended**

(A)   teachers
B   professors
C   students

5   **NOT MORE THAN THREE PASSENGERS**

A   bus drivers
(B)   taxi drivers
C   train drivers

Questions 6 – 10

Which notice (A – H) says this (6 – 10)?
For questions 6 – 10, mark the correct letter (A – H).

EXAMPLE	ANSWER
0 We make clothes.	H

6   You can get your hair done here.

7   We make furniture.

8   We work quickly.

9   You can get legal advice here.

10   We don't open in the morning.

A   **LAWYER'S OFFICE**

B   *Cut and blow dry £6.50*

C   **Best carpenter in town**

D   **Shoe repairs while you wait**

E   Office open 2pm–6pm

F   **EXPERT FURNITURE REPAIRS**

G   **Opening hours 8am – 12 noon**

H   **DRESSMAKERS**

Key

6 B   7 C   8 D   9 A   10 E

Part 2
Questions 11 – 15

Read the descriptions (11 – 15) of people who need something or someone.
Where do they need to go (A – H)?
For questions 11 – 15, mark the correct letter (A – H).

EXAMPLE	ANSWER
0 If you need oil for your car you buy it here.	F

11   People with toothache go there.

12   If you have a problem with your car you take it here.

13   You phone here if the central heating is broken.

14   If you feel ill you go there.

15   Only men have their hair cut here.

PLACES

A   garage

B   barber's

C   carpenter's

D   dentist's

E   electrician's

F   petrol station

G   hairdresser's

H   health centre

Key

11 D   **12** A   **13** E   **14** H   **15** B

Part 3
Questions 16 – 20

Complete the five conversations.
For questions 16 – 20, mark A, B or C.

EXAMPLE		ANSWER
0 Is your work interesting?	A Not very. B A lot. C Yes, he is.	A

16   Where do you work?

    (A)   In an office.
    B   Next year.
    C   I don't know.

17   What would you like to be?

    A   I like being a doctor.
    B   Yes, I would.
    (C)   A journalist.

18   How long have you worked there?

    A   8 hours a day.
    (B)   For 3 years.
    C   2 miles.

19   How much do you earn?

    A   Yes, very much.
    B   A long time.
    (C)   £1000 a month.

20   Do you like your job?

    A   I'd like to be a singer.
    B   I like dancing.
    (C)   No, I don't.

Questions 21 – 25

Complete the conversation
What does Jim say to Anne?
For questions 21 – 25, mark the correct letter (A – H).

EXAMPLE		ANSWER
Anne:	Hi, I haven't seen you since you got your new job. How's it going?	C
Jim:	0............	

Anne:	What's wrong? You don't look very happy. Don't you like it?	A	The problem is the boss.
Jim:	21 **G**	B	No, actually I'm well paid.
Anne:	Is it a hard job? Do you have to work very long hours?	C	Well, it's going OK.
Jim:	22 **H**	D	He's awful. He shouts all day long.
Anne:	Is the pay bad then? Do you earn very little?.	E	No, I win a lot of money.
Jim:	23 **B**	F	I like him a lot.
Anne:	I don't understand. What is the problem then?	G	Yes, I do like it but ...
Jim:	24 **A**	H	No, it isn't the hours.
Anne:	Oh dear! I didn't think of that. What's he like?		
Jim:	25 **D**		
Anne:	Poor Jim!		

Read the interview with the careers teacher.
Are sentences 26 – 32 'Right' (A) or 'Wrong' (B)?

If there is not enough information to answer 'Right' (A) or 'Wrong' (B),
choose 'Doesn't say' (C).

For questions 26 – 32, mark A, B or C.

Do you think we will get a job when we finish university?
Well, I can't promise that but I can give you some useful advice.

What is the first thing we should do?
First of all write a really good curriculum vitae with all the necessary information about yourself. The school you went to; your work experience; your hobbies and interests. Include a photograph.

What else is important?
It's very important to have some work experience. During your summer holidays try to find a job. If you are studying tourism for example, try to get a summer job in a hotel. The experience of working is more important than how much money you earn.

What about interviews?
Of course it's very important to arrive punctually and look smart. However, this is not enough. You should do more than just answer questions, you should also ask some questions and show interest in the job.

Is that all we need to know?
No, I think there is one more very important thing. A lot of young people say they can't get a job but in fact what they mean is that they can't get a job in their own town or near their own town. You must be prepared to travel to work or even live away from home. It's much easier to get the job you want if you are already working.

Thank you very much for answering our questions.
Not at all. I've enjoyed talking to you. Good luck with your careers.

EXAMPLE	ANSWER
0 The teacher isn't sure they will get a job when they finish their studies.	A
A Right B Wrong C Doesn't say	

26 A C.V. is the information you write about yourself when you are looking for a job.

(A) Right   B Wrong   C Doesn't say

27 It is important to earn a lot of money if you work

A Right   (B) Wrong   C Doesn't say

28 It is more important to arrive on time for an interview than to be well dressed.

A Right   (B) Wrong   C Doesn't say

29 During the interview you should only answer questions.

A Right   (B) Wrong   C Doesn't say

30 You should only look for work near your home.

A Right   (B) Wrong   C Doesn't say

31 If you have a job it is not so difficult to get another one.

(A) Right   B Wrong   C Doesn't say

32 You should be prepared to live away from home.

(A) Right   B Wrong   C Doesn't say

Read the article about work.
Choose the best word (A,B or C) for each space (33 – 40).
For questions 33 – 40, mark A, B or C.

━━━━ WORK ━━━━

Nowadays it is normal to work eight hours _0_ day in most countries *(a)* of the world. You cannot work legally _33_ you are _34_ sixteen *(if)* *(under)* years old.

Earlier this century, however, the situation _35_ very different. Very *(was)* young children _36_ very dangerous jobs. Children as young _37_ six *(did)* *(as)* years old worked in coalmines. People worked very long hours in extremely bad conditions and were very badly paid. Unfortunately, this _38_ happens in some countries. *(still)*

The main problems today are that many people _39_ got a job and *(haven't)* many _40_ work have to travel long distances to get there and so the *(who)* working day is still very long.

EXAMPLE			ANSWER
0 A in	B a	C the	B

33   A until   (B) if   C unless

34 (A) under   B down   C for

35 (A) was   B were   C went

36 (A) did   B done   C made

37   A so   (B) as   C than

38   A yet   B even   (C) still

39 (A) haven't   B don't   C won't

40   A what   (B) who   C why

Part 6
Questions 41 – 50

Complete these letters.
Write one word for each space (41 – 50).

Dear Mr Matthews

I am (Example: **sorry**) I cannot come __41__ work this week.
I __42__ got a very bad backache. The doctor says I __43__
stay in bed __44__ a week.

If you __45__ me to do some work in bed please send me a
note. (I can't answer the telephone!)

Sorry,

Richard

Dear Richard

Don't worry. I don't want you to work __46__ bed, I want you
to __47__ better __48__ .

I will come to see __49__ after work __50__ Wednesday.

Yours

Mr Matthews

Key

41 to **42** have **43** must **44** for **45** want/need
46 in **47** get/be **48** soon **49** you **50** on/next

Part 7
Questions 51 – 55

Read this information about a man who is applying for an office job.
Fill in the information on the job application.

Paul Topping is 20 years old and he is looking for a job in an
office. He has worked in another office since he was 17. He
is single. He likes his job but he would like to use computers
more. He has done a course in them.

JOB APPLICATION

First Name:		Paul
Surname:	51	Topping
Age:	52	20
Marital status:	53	Single
Years of experience:	54	3
Course/s in:	55	Computers

Part 8
Question 56

You have got a new job.

Write a note to a friend.

Explain:

<u>what</u> the job is

<u>when</u> you have to start and <u>how much</u> you will earn.

Write 20 – 25 words

LISTENING PAPER

Part 1
Questions 1 – 5

Listen to the tape.
You will hear five short conversations.
You will hear each conversation twice.
There is one question for each conversation.
For questions 1 – 5, put a tick ✓ under the right answer.

Here is an example:

EXAMPLE

0 What time is it?

0745   **0645**   **0715**

A ✓   B ☐   C ☐

---

1   Where is Jane's office?

At the traffic lights   **On the left**   **Opposite the cinema**

A ☐   B ☐   C ✓

2   When did Jane begin working there?

Two months ago In July   **In June**

A ✓   B ☐   C ☐

3   How much does Jane earn?

£850 a month   **£1,500 a month**   **£1,050 a month**

A ☐   B ✓   C ☐

4   What's the office like?

Large and new   **Big but old**   **Small but modern**

A ✓   B ☐   C ☐

5   Where does Jane have lunch?

In a cafe   **In a bar**   **In the office canteen**

A ☐   B ☐   C ✓

TAPESCRIPT

Test Five

Look at the instructions for Part One.
You will hear five, short conversations.
You will hear each conversation twice.
There is one question for each conversation.
For questions 1 – 5, put a tick under the right answer.
Here is an example:

Example: What time is it?
F   What's the time, Monica?
F   It's a quarter to eight.
F   Oh dear, I'm going to be late.   Can you give me a lift?
F   Of course I can, Jane
The answer is 7.45, so there is a tick in box A.
Now we are ready to start,
Look at question one,

One. Where is Jane's office?
F   How do I get there?
F   Go straight down this road to the traffic lights
F   Do I turn left or right at the traffic lights?
F   Turn left and my office is on the right, opposite the cinema.

Now listen again.

Two. When did she begin working there?
F   How long have you worked there now?
F   Let me see, this is July - I began in May
F   Do you enjoy your work?
F   Yes, a lot.

Now listen again.

Three. How much does Jane earn?
F   What about the money, Jane?
F   It's really good, I earn £1,500 a month
F   I only get £850 - you're lucky
F   I know!

Now listen again.

Four. What's the office like?
F   Is the office nice?
F   Yes, it's lovely - it's big and modern.
F   Do they need any more secretaries?
F   I'll let you know if they do!

Now listen again.

Five. Where does Jane have lunch?
F   Do you have lunch in a cafe?
F   No, the cafes and bars are very expensive around here.
F   Do you bring sandwiches, then?
F   No, we've got our own canteen.
F   Oh! That's great.

Now listen again

This is the end of Part One.

TAPESCRIPT

Now look at Part Two.

Listen to Lucy talking about what jobs she would or would not like to do.
Lucy talks about six jobs.
What does she need for each of these jobs?

For questions 6 – 10, write a letter (A – H) next to each job.
You will hear the conversation twice.

Sally: What are you going to do Lucy?

Lucy: I don't know. The jobs I could do I don't like and the ones I like, I can't.

Sally: What do you mean?

Lucy: Well, I can type and use computers but I don't want to work in an office. I've got A'levels so I could work in a bank but I wouldn't like that either.

Sally: What would you like?

Lucy: Well, I'd love to be a reporter but you need a university degree now. I'd quite like to be an air hostess too but I don't speak any French, Spanish or German...only English.

Sally: Isn't there anything else you like?

Lucy: Teaching would be OK I suppose but that's even more difficult, you need a degree and a teaching diploma.

Sally: What about working in a shop?

Lucy: I could do that but the pay isn't very good. Anyway, they always prefer some-one who has already worked in a shop before.

Sally: Poor Lucy!

Now listen again.

This is the end of Part Two.

Part 2
Questions 6 – 10

Listen to Sally talking to Lucy about what jobs she would or would not like to do.
Lucy talks about six jobs.
What does she need for each of these jobs?

For questions 6 – 10, write a letter (A – H) next to each job.
You will hear the conversation twice.

EXAMPLE	ANSWER
0 Office clerk	B

JOB		WHAT YOU NEED
6 Bank clerk	☐	A experience
		B typing and computer studies
7 Reporter	☐	C A levels
8 Air hostess	☐	D G.C.S.Es
		E languages
9 Teacher	☐	Γ a degree
		G teaching experience
10 Shop assistant	☐	H a degree and a diploma

Key

6 C   7 F   8 E   9 H   10 A

Part 3
Questions 11 – 15

Listen to Miss James at a job interview.

For questions 11 – 15, tick ✓ A, B or C.
You will hear the conversation twice.

EXAMPLE				ANSWER
0	Miss James can speak	A	5 foreign languages ✓	A
		B	3 foreign languages ☐	
		C	2 foreign languages ☐	

11   Her mother is   A   English.   ☐

                                       (B)   Spanish.   ✓

                                       C   French.   ☐

12   She learnt Russian   (A)   at school.   ✓

                                       B   at university.   ☐

                                       C   in Russia.   ☐

13   The hotel is called   A   Montara.   ☐

                                       (B)   Montana.   ✓

                                       C   Montena.   ☐

14   She worked there for   A   4 years.   ☐

                                       B   4 summers.   ☐

                                       (C)   4 months.   ✓

15   She could begin work   (A)   next week.   ✓

                                       B   after the interview.   ☐

                                       C   on Monday.   ☐

TAPESCRIPT

Now look at Part Three.
Listen to Miss James at a job interview.
For questions 11 – 15, tick A, B or C.
You will hear the conversation twice.
Look at questions 11 – 15 now. You have twenty seconds.
Now listen to the conversation.

Interviewer:	Good afternoon Miss James. Please sit down.
Miss James:	Thank you.
Interviewer:	Now, I looked at your application and it's one of the best ones we've received. I see you speak Spanish, French, German, Italian and even a little Russian!
Miss James:	Well, I'm lucky because my mother is Spanish. My father is English but he works for an international company so when I was young I lived for a few years in France and then in Germany.
Interviewer:	What about Italian and Russian? Where did you learn those?
Miss James:	I studied Italian at school and at university but Russian just at school.
Interviewer:	Why did you choose to study tourism?
Miss James:	Because I love languages and I like meeting people from different countries.
Interviewer:	I also see you worked in a hotel in London last summer the ... Montara.
Miss James:	The Montana - M O N T A N A not R A.
Interviewer:	Right. How long did you work there?
Miss James:	All summer, June, July, August and September.
Interviewer:	Mmm, Miss James if you got a job in our hotel, when could you start? Next week perhaps?
Miss James:	After this interview if you like!

LAUGHTER

Now listen again.

This is the end of Part Three.

TAPESCRIPT

Part Four.

You will hear a girl speaking on the telephone.
She wants to speak to Paul but he is not there.

Listen and complete questions 16 – 20.
You will hear the information twice.

M   892 8360

F   Hello, is Paul in please?

M   No, I'm sorry he's not. Can I take a message?

F   Yes please. Could you tell him Amanda phoned.

M   Oh it's you, Amanda. I didn't recognise your voice. How are you?

F   I'm fine, Mr Wilson. Well, actually I'm very happy. I've just got a new job and that's why I'm phoning.

M   That's very good news. Do you want me to tell Paul?

F   No, please don't. I would like to tell him myself tonight. Could you ask him to meet me outside the pub at 8 o'clock, no sorry at 8.30 because there's a lot of traffic on Friday.

M   Is there anything else?

F   Just one thing. Tell him to wear trousers, not jeans. I'm taking him to an expensive restaurant.

M   All right, I'll tell him. Have a lovely time.

F   Thanks a lot. Bye.

M   Goodbye.

Now listen again.

This is the end of Part Four.

Part 4
Questions 16 – 20

Listen to a girl speaking on the telephone.
She wants to speak to Paul, but he is not there.

For questions 16 – 20, complete the message to Paul.
You will hear the conversation twice.

MESSAGE

To:	**Paul**
From:	(16) **Amanda**
Meet her outside the:	(17) **pub**
At:	(18) **8.30**
Wear:	(19) **trousers**
Going to have dinner in:	(20) **an expensive restaurant**

Listen to some information about evening classes.

For questions 21 – 25, complete the information about the evening classes.
You will hear the information twice.

EVENING CLASSES

Classes from:	_7 p.m._
To:	(21) _10 p.m._
Students must be over:	(22) _16 years old_
Spanish classes cost:	(23) _£50_
Advanced computer courses on Tuesday and:	(24) _Thursday_
Computer classes cost:	_£75_
Maximum number of students in French classes:	(25) _15_

TAPESCRIPT

Now look at Part Five.
You will hear some information about some evening classes.
Listen and complete questions 21-25.
You will hear the information twice.

Thank you for calling West Meade College. This is a recorded message.

There are classes every evening from 7 p.m. to 10 p.m. These classes are only for people over 16 years old. The language courses, Spanish or French, are on Monday, Wednesday and Friday for beginners from 8 to 9 p.m. and on Tuesday and Thursday from 8.30 to 10 p.m. for people who already know some Spanish or French. These courses cost £50 per person.

There is a computer studies course on Monday, Wednesday and Friday from 7 to 8 p.m. and an advanced course on Tuesday and Thursday from 7 to 8 p.m. These courses cost £75.

There is also an English literature course on Friday from 8 to 10 p.m. which costs £55.

The maximum number of students per class is 15 for Spanish, French and English literature and 20 for computer studies.

Classes begin on Monday 15th and Tuesday 16th September, except for English literature which begins on Friday 19th.

If you need any more information please phone 817 1911.

Now listen again.

This is the end of Part Five.

Richmond Publishing
19 Berghem Mews
Blythe Road
London W14 OHN

© Susan McGeary 1995

First published by Richmond Publishing® 1995
Reprinted 1996

ISBN: 84–294–4666–4

Author's Acknowledgement

Thanks to Min for typing the manuscript and to my mother
for researching signs in England.

Printed in Spain by Gráfica Internacional, S.A.
D.L.: M-5.342-1996